Debbie Frank's

Cosmic Ordering Guide to Life, Love & Happiness

Debbie Frank pens the astrology sections of the *Daily Mirror*, the *Sunday Mirror* and *First* magazine. Debbie has been an astrologer for over twenty years, and she supported Princess Diana through the last eight traumatic years of her life. Debbie's a Scorpio and lives in London with her husband and daughter.

Visit her website at *www.debbiefrank.co.uk*

Debbie Frank's

Cosmic Ordering Guide to Life, Love & Happiness

Change Your Life in a Moment

PENGUIN BOOKS

PENGUIN BOOKS

Published by the Penguin Group

Penguin Books Ltd, 80 Strand, London WC2R 0RL, England

Penguin Group (USA) Inc., 375 Hudson Street,
New York, New York 10014, USA

Penguin Group (Canada), 90 Eglinton Avenue East, Suite 700,
Toronto, Ontario, Canada M4P 2Y3 (a division of Pearson Penguin Canada Inc.)

Penguin Ireland, 25 St Stephen's Green, Dublin 2, Ireland
(a division of Penguin Books Ltd)

Penguin Group (Australia), 250 Camberwell Road, Camberwell,
Victoria 3124, Australia (a division of Pearson Australia Group Pty Ltd)

Penguin Books India Pvt Ltd, 11 Community Centre,
Panchsheel Park, New Delhi – 110 017, India

Penguin Group (NZ), 67 Apollo Drive, Mairangi Bay, Auckland 1310,
New Zealand (a division of Pearson New Zealand Ltd)

Penguin Books (South Africa) (Pty) Ltd, 24 Sturdee Avenue,
Rosebank, Johannesburg 2196, South Africa

Penguin Books Ltd, Registered Offices: 80 Strand, London WC2R 0RL, England

www.penguin.com

First published 2007
1

Set in Galliard
Typeset by seagulls.net
Printed in England by Clays Ltd, St Ives plc

ISBN: 978–0–141–03089–0

To Lulu-Mei – you are my
very special delivery!

Contents

Introduction

What if ...

Why did I write this book? Being an astrologer, I have had all sorts of people confide in me over the years about their hopes, dreams and wishes. I have heard stories of great fulfilment and major disappointment. It is wonderful when somebody feels that they are getting what they want or the stars are perfectly aligned, or they feel in tune with what the universe has to offer or that a dream has come true. It happens. Yet also I frequently hear people saying they've had a raw deal, they don't know what they're doing wrong or they never meet anyone.

It's true there is an order to the cosmos that is beyond our control. But we can also *make* a cosmic order. Suddenly, everyone's becoming aware of this – people are talking about cosmic ordering and putting their wishes out to the universe.

But then what? What if nothing happens? What if the universe still doesn't deliver? This book addresses the 'What ifs'. It will help you to see that *you* are the one who creates your reality. It is not that you need to change what you are or are not doing. You have to address the beliefs and patterns that are keeping hold of your cosmic order down at the depot, rather than having it couriered straight to your door!

'All that we are is a result of what we have thought.'
Buddha

As an astrologer I'm always asked, 'What's going to happen to me?' The question implies that the cosmos has it all mapped out for you. People are taken aback when I reply, 'What do you *wish* your future to be?' *Because eventually you become what you think.* Our thoughts are incredibly powerful – they are like viruses that spread so rapidly they impact on everything we do. How we think not only influences events in our lives, but also determines how we experience these events, what we attract and what we make of it all.

So if what we're thinking is such a big deal, then it's essential to put in the right thoughts. If we think positively then we can actively use this amazing facility, this ordering device, this delivery service. We can request all sorts of things – an opportunity, a relationship, a greater sense of happiness. This doesn't have to be an ego trip either – you can also ask for someone else's happiness, or wish them well in life. But is it really going to work? Can a wish make a difference? So often I hear people say, 'I never meet anyone. I never get offered what I want.' What's going on?

Are You Ready to Order?

If you go to a restaurant and the waiter comes to take your order you wouldn't dream of saying 'steak and chips' if what you really wanted to eat was salmon and new potatoes. Cosmic ordering is just like going to a restaurant and placing your order. The whole technique is so simple. Ask for what you want, not what you don't want. Don't mention the things you're leaving aside; just pick out the very thing you want most at that moment.

In a restaurant, if a waiter is slow in taking your order you have to attract his attention. It's the same with the cosmos. Sometimes you need to be very up-front, using your willpower to get yourself noticed and to get what you want. At other times the service is slow, it goes at its own pace, but you are enjoying the ambience and can go with the flow until whatever it is you want arrives.

Sometimes you order what you want but something different arrives. The cosmos may send you someone or something you didn't expect. You may choose to send it back, or you might think, 'Actually, this is rather good, I'll have it!'

Are Things Meant to Be?

So, are things 'meant to be'? Does fate deal us a hand? To a certain extent, yes. We are not blank slates. We come in with some things already written yet it's what we chalk up that counts. We can't choose what we are born into (or maybe we can, but that's another spiritual theory). We can, however, always choose what we think and how we deal with things. Our influence over reality seems very subtle to us, but it is actually hugely significant.

If a solid object, such as a spoon, can be bent using the power of the mind, then reality isn't nearly as stable or immoveable as it seems. Everything is in the process of change at some level. *We interact with fate all the time*. Sometimes we think of ourselves as powerless to do anything, and that's when circumstances dictate what happens. Sometimes we block things. We try to take control and thereby avoid a difficulty. But in doing so we are refusing to open up or to look at another perspective and might prevent ourselves from receiving the good things in life.

Wish

I wrote this book because I believe that there is more to cosmic ordering than simply making a wish. There is more to astrology then the subtle energies of the stars. *You are the vital ingredient. The one who holds the power.* I've written about your patterns, the things that get in the way of cosmic ordering, and about how you can think differently, act in a powerful way and make your wishes come true. At this moment you are already magnetizing your own reality. This book has come into your hands, either by choice or by 'accident'. Create what you want with these words, I wish you the best for life, love and happiness.

1
The Universe –
Two Worlds Colliding

The Visible World

We each have a different take on life, love and the universe. We see things through our own lens so that no one else's reality exactly matches ours. Of course we all agree that a spade is a spade, a plate a plate. But even these objects are not as solid as they might at first appear. They are made up of tiny vibrating particles that hang together in a shape that we see and touch, and understand to be a spade, a plate. All things in our physical everyday world, including the food we eat, the clothes we wear and our own bodies, are all made up of the same stuff – energy.

When looking at life, it's important not to accept things at face value. We are constantly hearing the scientific view: that something can only exist if it is proved. So it's amazing that even though love and beauty can't be proved they are real enough to us.

The extraordinary thing is that no scientist has been able to prove that the so-called 'real world' actually exists. The world looks real enough, but under microscopic examination it turns out to be a force field of raw electromagnetic energy that arranges itself into shapes and patterns that we recognize and which register in our brains as various identifiable objects.

So you could say that we actually manufacture the world inside our heads, as our bodies and brains receive messages and our five senses organize impressions about what's out there, and we process the information into our dear old familiar world. Ah, there it is again. We repeat the sights, sounds and signals to ourselves and are re-assured that we still exist, that everything is still there and is still the same.

Except it isn't.

The real wow factor to come out of all this is that we create our own reality and we choose to see what we want to see. We each shape and choose our own version of reality through our individual filters, which are our qualities as a human being, our expectations and our environment.

This is a very liberating thought. It means that we are not limited to experiencing life as 'what happens to us'. **The universe is in fact a reflection of you. As such you can change or rearrange it into a shape that suits you.**

Now this might sound as if it requires a magic trick, or years of yogic discipline. But actually there is nothing unusual about it. You already do it. You are already seeing the world through your own views, ideas, tastes, conditioning and awareness. And it looks very different to you in comparison with the next person.

The Invisible World

There is an invisible world that infiltrates every aspect of our being. This world is what glues everything together and helps us to make sense of life. It contains our feelings, our hunches, our knowledge, our connections with others. It is what Jung called 'the collective' and what Deepak Chopra calls 'the soup'.

Some people feel more connected to this invisible realm than others. Doctors, scientists and engineers tend to be fascinated by what they see in tangible terms in the visible world, while media types, artists and writers will often be drawn to the invisible. But, putting that aside, we are each of us positioned somewhere on the spectrum and we shift between the two extremes.

We are forced to live in the 'real' visible world because we have been born into it. We live in our body, which is our first tangible asset. Dealing with the physical is an essential ingredient of life. We all have to accept the inescapable real world: deal with money, find a place to live, get food to eat and perform various bodily functions. And the world we discover could be a place of beauty, pleasure and enjoyment. Some of the physical functions are very pleasant indeed!

The invisible world, on the other hand, is optional – it may seem like a luxury, but it's not a holiday island where we can go and indulge ourselves. We repress or deny it at our peril. You may recognize feelings of bottled-up anger or frustration. Imagine how far and wide your negative energy has travelled before you do finally blow.

The invisible realm is where we find our guidance, inspiration, love, kindness, acceptance and forgiveness, and also our sense that something big is about to happen. The invisible realm gets a lot of knocks from the hard-core real-world fraternity. As if it doesn't exist. Which is fair enough as it *is* invisible! But just wait until one of these rational types of people falls in love. Then they realize there is more to life than facts and figures. But, of course, the scientists have got their hands on love too, recently announcing it is no more than a bunch of chemicals being released into our bloodstream. They say we are really at the mercy of a quick hit of seratonin or whatever. This may be true at a biochemical level, but it's also the spiritual, emotional, out-of-this-world, feel-good factor that connects two souls, and love cannot be reduced to the level of a few hyped-up chemicals on the loose.

Good or Bad? Reality is Not Objective

The invisible realm joins us together. When clients come to see me as an astrologer and I start explaining about a particular transit of a planet on their chart, they will often interrupt and demand to know, 'Is it good or bad?' This sums up how disturbing it is for us to embrace any invisible force without us immediately wanting to organize it – before it's even happened – into something manageable and definable. That's how we take control. Or we think we do.

In the invisible reality what happens to us shouldn't be categorized in this way, because out of the worst experiences comes the most awareness, and the surfacing of inner strength. Sometimes the 'good' experiences that we look forward to, such as marriage or the birth of a baby, can also be the most stressful. Nothing is as it seems or as it is expected to be. It is all just part of the whole.

Every situation can be viewed as good or bad depending on who's doing the viewing. In fact this either/or mentality can be extremely wearing. We can be very quick to judge. This is the kind of attitude that can lead to division, divorce, and even to wars. So just when you're about to attack someone with all the force of an emotional terrorist, it's good to remember that each of us is made up of the same stuff (visible world) and that we are all connected (invisible world).

No matter how separate, isolated or lonely you feel, whether you choose to go off and meditate in silence in a mountain hut for twenty years or lie in bed all day with a migraine it is simply impossible to be disconnected. *You are part of the soup whether you want to be or not.*

Whether you choose to have your closest friends on speed-dial is entirely up to you. Having people available to you through the five senses and technology gives you a presence of sorts. But spending time seeing, talking to or exchanging emails with people is not the only way to maintain connection.

A baby learns that his parents still love him and will care for him even when he is alone at night in a cot. He has to develop a trust in the invisible world – for example, with the help of a transitional object he is able to hold on to the love of his parents even when temporarily they are not present. If we had never learnt this then we would literally be tied to our mother's apron strings well into our mid-life crisis.

The truth is that we often connect with one another through thought. Sometimes that thought is received so strongly by the other person that he or she picks up the phone and rings.

Energy

Which brings us on to energy. By that I don't mean food calories, or what you expend on the treadmill or by running after your child or your lover. I mean the energy which is the stuff of life in the invisible realm and is the very thing that we pick up on without even realizing.

This kind of energy comes in different weights and forces. It can be a heavy force that lumbers about like an elephant, towers high as a block of flats or fills the air in the form of a black mood. In contrast, light energy can be like fine cotton, a feather or a kiss.

We feel the energy of another person even though it's invisible. It's what attracts us to particular people, makes us move away from others, and in some cases (if we are especially permeable) seems to make us take on the moods of others and then wonder why we feel the way we do. Feeling the energy, the mood, the atmosphere, the vibration – whatever you want to call it – requires you to notice and pick up on the subtle forces and currents that swirl around places, people and situations.

The more you are aware of this energy, the easier it is to understand what's going on, time your moves and get your cosmic orders out into a receptive atmosphere.

● How We Can Change the Energy or the Experience

Since the world arranges itself around our expectations, we can make a difference to it by changing them. For instance, if you expect a particular person of your acquaintance to be awash with self-pity, or greedy and demanding, then that is exactly what they will be. But if you see them each time you meet as if for the first time, with fresh eyes and zero expectations, then you are giving them the opportunity to surprise you.

I could go as far as to add that the mere fact of our presence in a room filled with inanimate objects would change the energy of that room. That the minute we observe something it loses its previous essence, because the act of us being present and noticing it has changed the energy.

WE ASK FOR SOMETHING IN A SPIRITUAL SENSE

But the delivery is earthly! Cosmic ordering is a connection between heaven and earth, the divine and the mundane.

Understanding the Universe in Terms of Cosmic Ordering

It's important to open your energy channels and to be receptive, aware and available to receiving signals from the invisible world – both those we receive from other people, and those we pick up on that confirm to us that we are on the right track, in the right place or on to something.

The whole point is not to be asleep on this great journey called life, but to be alert to the messages that are available. To make sure that you are conscious enough to make an order, and awake for the delivery, no matter what time it comes.

You need to notice your own energy, your life force. Become aware of the ebb and flow, and of how much impact certain people and situations have upon it. How can you reinforce your energy and protect yourself against energy-sappers? You need to be strong in body and mind, bright-eyed and bushy-tailed to receive the benefits of cosmic ordering.

The whole process means that you can't afford just to sit back and let life happen to you. Sure, there are currents out there that could cause you to drift from time to time. But you need to steer a course, and have a purpose or a destination in mind. Saying yes to life involves making sure you're aware of and using everything that's available to you.

When you feel down, or are worried, you immediately put a stop to the flow of energy. In fact, there is a great deal of truth in the saying that you are your own worst enemy. Every time you think a negative thought, assume the worst or buy into the group mentality that's operating on fear then you lose energy. That's not to say that thinking or talking about 'bad' things will always create negative energy. It's true that a problem shared can be a problem halved. But it can also mean a problem doubled. If you can come through those thoughts or conversations with something positive, or if you can help someone through positive listening (but not magnifying) then you are opening yourself up to good energy, to solutions or to a feeling of release.

The Concept of Abundance and Flow

Never hesitate to choose to give of yourself freely. Be generous with your love, ideas and gestures of kindness. Give of yourself – that is the greatest gift. You will never run out, and the more you give the more you can manifest. Out there in the invisible realm is enough of everything to create whatever you are capable of imagining, so don't be stingy when it comes to giving it out.

But you also need to be generous with yourself. Which means *relaxing* where possible. Not chasing after things, running around, or trying desperately hard. If you take the effort out of doing things it means that the flow can be restored. Worrying yourself silly that there won't be enough of what you want, or you will never fulfil your desires, or things won't be good enough, simply clogs up your energy system and therefore can be a self-fulfilling prophecy.

The amazing thing about the universe is that it flows along without us. The key is to tap into the flow and be open to it. The clearer our thoughts and desires, the easier it is to harness. In the next chapter you will discover just what cosmic ordering is and how the universe can respond.

2
What is
Cosmic Ordering?

What is It?

Cosmic ordering is the new buzzword for something which has been around for years in the form of positive visualization. That said, people still constantly ask me, 'What exactly is it?' Simply put, cosmic ordering involves asking for some help from 'the powers that be' in order to make your wishes and desires come true. It requires intention, belief, a desire to break patterns from the past and the capacity to spot and take advantage of opportunities.

Who Do You Ask?

The universe is non-denominational and does not mind what you call it or how you do your ordering. All that matters is that you are able to communicate your desires and your hopes, and to focus on getting them delivered.

What It is Not

This may all sound wonderful: that you can ask to win the lottery, become as rich as Croesus and spend the rest of your days wherever you wish, courtesy of the private jet and millions of pounds' worth of super-yacht. You can dream up the perfect lover, zoom up to the top job and become one of the A-list. Cosmic ordering doesn't preclude any of this from happening, but it works best when you see it as a powerful tool to help you transform your life rather than as a cop-out cosmic wish list and mail-order delivery service.

The energy involved in cosmic ordering cannot be used to harm other people, or to get what you want at someone else's expense. It is essentially a benign influence that can be tapped into.

Nor is cosmic ordering a panacea. For instance, it can't magically make you recover from a serious illness. There are many stories where people have gone into remission through 'sheer willpower' or 'positive thinking' – but that's another book in itself and I wouldn't want to make any sweeping statements suggesting that cosmic ordering can right the world's wrongs. It is a way of tuning into the *best available* opportunities for you.

Fate and Free Will

The debate between fate and free will is similar to the one between nature and nurture – both are vast subjects that refuse to conform to a perfect answer.

Do we determine our lives through the use of willpower, and are we totally free to do so? Or does fate lend a hand – do we have a destiny that is born the moment we first draw breath? I like to think life is an interplay between fate and free will. We are all born with a set of building blocks that is unique to each of us. What we choose to make of it is our decision. On the other hand, we may attract events and people into our lives that we prefer to think of as due to fate.

Where does fate begin? When the chromosomes arrange themselves so that we lean towards certain qualities and characteristics? Some spiritual thinking argues that we choose our talents, our childhood conditions and our relationships before we are born. But, even so, there may be scope to change the experience via free will.

How to Put in a Cosmic Order

The truth is there is no correct way to do it. But whichever way you do choose to communicate with the cosmos needs to fit in with your beliefs and feel right for you. You might want to meditate, listen to music, write down your wishes in a private journal, or say them out loud like a prayer. You might have a special time of the day or a particular place that feels still enough for you to sense the connection with the cosmos. But you don't have to sit cross-legged, burn incense or become a yogi to do it. If you feel like putting in a cosmic order while driving, or as you push a trolley round the supermarket, that's fine. The important thing is that you do it in a heartfelt way. You can even visualize sending a cosmic order like you would send a text or an email. (This can also work with unwanted thoughts that go round and round in your head – simply press the delete button!)

Gold-star Cosmic Ordering

Timing is notoriously difficult – the universe doesn't necessarily respond with a same-day delivery. But you can boost your chances by practising 'gold-star cosmic order-ing', which is a highly concentrated version of the standard kind. It involves putting in your order with a much greater degree of passion and conviction. So instead of idly thinking, 'It would be nice if such-and-such happened', you actively engage yourself with the process 110 per cent, body and soul. You don't just make a wish, but you visualize yourself having already achieved whatever it is you desire. You see yourself having/being/doing your wish in the present tense. Strangely, the universe seems to know whether you expect to get what you want, or whether you have a sneaking suspicion that you won't, or whether you're wondering if you really deserve it or if it's not possible at all.

So you might be writing down your orders, but each time you place one you are thinking to yourself, 'This whole process is a bit odd, isn't it? I wonder if cosmic ordering really works.'

I was made aware of the non-verbal clues that deliver messages of intention when I signed up to do a morning at the horse school, which is part of the Miraval Spa in Arizona. Most of my group had no previous experience, but we were each assigned a horse to groom and school. Firstly, as we watched the instructor show us how it was done, it seemed easy, and his horse obligingly responded to everything he wanted it to do.

Then it was our turn – starting with cleaning up our horses' hooves. I was handed the tool to do the job, and my horse, which had never met me before, was tethered facing in the opposite direction. So how could I get this horse to pick up its foot? That's when I realized that I was at a total loss as to how to make this animal do what I wanted it to. Words were useless. Showing it the tool, touching its leg – both generated no response.

As the instructor came around he told us to move towards the horse's leg with conviction. To stop doubting whether the horse would co-operate. He asked us to imagine it happening and to hold the picture of it in our minds. Horses pick up all the non-verbal clues: they get their instruction from your body language, and will take no notice if you dither and act as if you don't know what you're doing. The moment I held the intention more powerfully, hey presto, that hoof came up to be cleaned.

I learnt from that little episode that how you hold yourself and convey your intentions really does matter. The universe, like the horse, also responds to clear intentions better than to maybes. A big breakthrough in your mission to get your desires met is to *act as if* it has already happened. Then you will adopt the posture, the mindset and the emotional responses that go with the fulfilment of that wish. And, as energy attracts energy, you're more likely to get that cosmic order delivered. You can expect gold-star service from the cosmos if you're putting in gold-star orders, without misleading information, doubts or confusion. The more committed you are, the easier it is to overcome any resistance around you.

How many times have you heard someone say, 'Well, I had good intentions, but …' Unless you keep the outcome in mind then the energy for it just slips away, disappears and evaporates into the cosmos.

Becoming a Magnet

In fact, this heading is a misnomer, as *you already are a magnet*. Without realizing it, you attract everything into your life by virtue of who you are and by what you are thinking, imagining, speaking about and doing. The universe is always reflecting yourself back to you, so that much of what happens to you is a mirror of how you've been feeling – what you've been worrying about or where you've been positive and upbeat. To a great extent character is destiny. We are constantly creating vibes that draw various experiences to us.

It's so easy to think that you're not responsible for what happens. And in some cases clearly you are not. But in the free will versus fate debate you have to take a 50:50 hit and at least own up to being involved in the process of generating your life. Some people like to think of themselves as scriptwriters choosing to invent a new plot-line, character or love interest. Or we can think of it as instant karma – where our actions sow the seeds of the outcome.

● Keeping Out the Negative

It's always important to keep visualizing what you want, instead of running worst-case scenarios through in your head. If you are continually fixating on not having something or someone then the energy is sent into a spiral and has nothing to do except send you more of the same. **You need to expect to receive.** Remember, whenever you are worrying, as far as the universe is concerned you are still in the planning stage – so stop that immediately!

It's also important to learn how to *protect yourself* from other people's negative vibrations and from the general dross that's out there. It's so easy to be put off by those who scoff at you, or who secretly don't want you to get what you want. Why don't they want you to move forward? Because you then undermine their own position, and they may have invested heavily in life staying the same. If you meet the right person, or become much more fulfilled and happy, in their eyes you will leave them behind. Don't take their feelings personally, by the way. That's a great protection in itself.

● When Things Feel Right

If we open ourselves up to noticing the little signals in the universe then we'll see when confirmation is flagged up. Someone we know will lend us the book that tells us more about what we want to do, or we'll read an article 'by chance' that helps us make the next move. We feel good about our choices and wishes from the thought right down to the gut instinct.

● Active Waiting

With cosmic ordering it's also good to realize there is such a thing as *actively waiting*. What this means is that you fully intend to get a result, but are aware that you need to read the signals, currents, timing and conditions.

This is different from simply waiting – where you give up your own will and power, and hand over responsibility to the cosmos to deliver. Using intention is like exercising a muscle – you need to go to the mind-gym and practise using it in your everyday life in order to make it stronger.

When the Universe Fails to Deliver

What if you've put in your cosmic order and the universe hasn't sent it recorded delivery, or you weren't available

33 ● ● ●

for signing when the courier called, or it has simply gone astray in the post? Does that mean that you won't ever get it? That you should give up, because cosmic ordering doesn't work? You might start asking yourself if it's meant to be, if it's right for you or whether there's something more sinister at work. Like deep down you feel you don't deserve it, or you're not ready for it. Chapter six shows you how to shift any blocks which might be preventing your order from getting through.

Are We Entitled?

The issue with cosmic ordering is that we can mistakenly believe that we are entitled to get whatever we want. We can also get *fixated on* and *obsessed about* our desire. We can't stop thinking about it; we are compulsively drawn to the idea of being with someone or getting what we want. We are so *attached to this desire* that we actually block off the flow of energy and we lose our ability to relax. Being so uptight about it puts cosmic ordering into reverse. We demand that the cosmos delivers and satisfies our ego as if it is our right to have whatever we want. But it doesn't work that way.

Sometimes you want something, but it simply isn't the right time for it to happen. You sometimes have to *let go* of the time frame and allow the universe to get on with delivering at its own pace. Or maybe you've asked for something and don't realize that the universe has acknowledged the order and is trying to send it to you, but you can't recognize it because the person/job/house doesn't appear how you expected. In this case, maybe your specifics need a rethink. Perhaps it's time to break out of old patterns when it comes to relationships and open up to being with a different kind of person. The same goes for changing career or living somewhere else.

There is a lot to be said for simply *relaxing* and *trusting* that the universe will do its best to deliver your cosmic order, subject to stocks, availability and the absolute rightness of the order: i.e. whether or not it will fit into the grand scheme of things. Extending your search parameters to focus more on the quality of what you want, rather than its material substance, is a brilliant way to get cosmic ordering to work for you. If you focus on your desire to be happy and feel powerful, rather than getting a red Maserati, then it's an order that the universe can fulfil in whatever way is possible.

Inevitably you cut yourself off from a lot of perfectly good possibilities by being very picky or too specific about the details. Also, dare I say that maybe we don't always know exactly what's good or right for us. The important thing is that you are able to create that magnetic energy or attraction and direct it towards the kinds of things or people that will enhance your life in some way.

You Don't Have to Manage the Process

Developing trust and a positive attitude isn't as easy as it sounds, because we live in a world that seems to operate on the need to be in control. You can even say that putting in a cosmic order is an attempt to maintain a degree of control. But there is always a mystery x factor – we can't control everything in our lives. There is a mysterious process at work that introduces us to some experiences but not to others. This is the interplay between fate and free will – more of that later. But we can assume that the universe has some kind of intelligence, that there is meaning in what we encounter and that we don't live a totally random life that is full of chaos and incidents that are slung together without any coherent intention.

For instance, we may spend a lot of time wondering how we can be with x if he or she is already with someone else. Or how we could go to Fiji if all our funds are already allocated. But the more uptight we get in trying to arrange everything and work it all out, then the more stagnant the energy becomes. We need to be able to fall back into the flow, relax, take it easy, and let the universe in its wisdom relieve us of the burden.

We don't have to resolve all the issues or try so hard to make it work. We don't have to bash our heads against a brick wall. We can be more Buddhist in attitude and serenely accept our current situation, while hoping for the best and thinking positively. We don't have to make a snatch-and-grab raid on what we want. Or continually fight off the competition, or struggle so hard. If we can get into the flow then our whole energy changes. We can just focus our attention on expecting a positive outcome and stop getting so engrossed and involved in the details that send us into a negative spin. Sometimes we are so wrapped up in the parameters of a problem that it becomes truly impossible to resolve. We can only solve it by developing the kind of awareness that lets us get beyond it. We outgrow the problem; it is no longer a big deal.

Being Awake and Alert

Being awake and conscious is a crucial element of successful cosmic ordering. If you go around half-asleep and don't really notice what's going on in your life, who's there and what it's all about, then, unsurprisingly, it's hard for the universe to get through to you. You might be asleep when the messenger calls! And you might be so sound asleep that you even fail to register what your night-time dreams have to say to you.

It's not as though just putting in a positive thought is going to overturn something that is deeply ingrained in our lives. We need to look at what we're all about, the messes we've got ourselves into, and to understand that successful cosmic ordering may require us to change our attitude to life. In other words – it's not totally up to the cosmos. We need to be personally involved, aware and ready.

● ● ●

In the next three chapters I'm going to focus on cosmic ordering for love and relationships. Love, same as cosmic ordering, is pretty hard to explain or prove. For some of us love seems like the hardest thing in life to find ... but that's all about to change.

3
The Attraction Factor

Cosmic Ordering for Love

● **Who are you attracting – and why?**

What is it that draws two people together? Is it fate or pheromones? Is it as simple as making a choice? Is it love at first sight? A compulsion or an unconscious pull? Is it even possible to bring someone into your life by putting in a cosmic order? Or to make a relationship better by sending your wishes out to the universe?

The law of attraction is only a mystery if we don't put any thought into how it might work. If we are to become aware of why certain people come into our lives, or don't as the case may be, then we need to understand what's going on beneath the surface. We need to discover what we are magnetizing, and what it is about us that keeps pulling in or pushing away particular people.

The first step is to ask yourself:

What are you putting out?

What are you getting back?

And what links the two?

Do you keep attracting the same kind of person?

What is your secret agenda?

WLTM

It's easy to say you *would like to meet* someone. But what kind of person? What do you really mean? Dating websites and personal ads are full of people seemingly wanting the same thing. GSOH (good sense of humour) seems to be a must, as is being fit, solvent and single. But if it really were that simple, and people were so easy to please, then why do so many of us find it

Are you desiring total oneness, openness, togetherness, acceptance, support and connection of souls, all in glorious blazing technicolour, with flashing lights and sexual attraction?

Are you addicted to longing? For the wonderful future person, or for the ex who got away?

difficult? Scratch the surface of your WLTM and you'll find a whole different agenda.

The more you siphon off your energy into dreams of the future or memories of the past, the less there is available for the here and now. The addiction to longing can also be hard to break. We enjoy feeling that our ideal relationship is in the future, that Mr or Miss Right will come along one day, and in the meantime we don't have to deal with a real relationship.

Do you feel let down by the endless disappointment?

Maybe you never get lift-off?

Are you in a long-lived relationship that fails to deliver its promise?

Or have you had a series of no-hopers: a pattern of people with different names and faces, who purport to being unique individuals, but end up blending into one distinctive theme in your life?

The amazing thing is that the similarities between these 'no-hopers' is not really to do with them, but with you! You are doing something to attract this kind of person. As they say – once is chance, twice is coincidence, three times is enemy action. Meaning there is something going on in your unconscious that invites this pattern, this type of person, whether you realize it or not.

Your Relationship Patterns

Has someone got their hooks into you? Maybe you don't even realize it. But on some level, deep down, you do see what's happening. It goes something like this: 'Here we are again, that's very alluring and very attractive, I recognize it, it's familiar, I'm at home with this one.'

Astoundingly, if we have a wobbly attachment to our parents we tend to recreate it in later life, because it feels familiar. So our attraction factor would go something like this: 'Oh yes, this person makes me feel insecure, I recognize this feeling from my childhood, this absence of positive love feels familiar, I'll go for it.' It looks crazy on paper. And of course you might be busy telling yourself and your friends that you're really looking for love, but underneath you're attracted to the lack of love that you have experienced before.

Then there's compulsion. When we feel instantly attracted, the power of the feelings are huge, but they are not necessarily going to generate a positive relationship. The symptoms of compulsion are a lack of freedom over your *choice*. Even having a 'type' implies there is some kind of hook or pattern at work that operates without you really choosing.

Unhooking yourself requires you to say 'no' to the habitual and to consider what you really want and need. To become aware. Give yourself some space to examine the pull before choosing. What is it? A cluster of desire energy? Or an old energy pattern overlaid with desire and compulsion? That instant chemical reaction might be good information that someone is a possibility for you – or it could be a hook that plays havoc with your biochemistry in the same way addiction would. The key is to be discriminating at the same time as remaining open.

The Mess in the Message!

We need to understand the effect our parents have had on us. Jung and Freud's take on our neuroses is rooted in what happened to us in early life. Whether we feel we had a 'normal', 'ideal' or 'difficult' childhood, this feeling has a lot to say about the potent image of our parents that we carry around in our psyche.

Even if our parents are long dead, or we don't feel close to them, we still cling on to their messages. They have a huge role to play in the creation of our love myths and messages, and in our love maps. The family is where we first learn about human relationships.

Whatever messages we are fed or pick up on about love in our childhood form our *personal attraction factor*. We can stay in its grip and be perfectly happy with it, but if we do want to change it we can – it doesn't have to control us. But the first step is to become aware of what it is. We need to find out who is in there, inside us, telling us what to think, how to behave and what we want. We need to know which parent's message is blueprinting our current relationship or our search for one.

The similarities, threads and patterns you find being repeated in every relationship are not really anything to do with the relationship itself – they are all about you. Your choices, your personal magnetism, and your unconscious blueprint and behaviour.

Ticking the Boxes

When answering the questions below you need to do so from the perspective of your impression of what happened in your parents' relationship. It's **your impression** that counts. It doesn't matter whether your brother or sister would agree with you, or if you're not sure that's what your mother would say about herself.

The important insight to gain from this exercise is to see how you perceive your parents, what message they handed down to you and how their relationship has shaped you.

☑ What message did your mother give you about love?

☑ What message did your father give you about love?

☑ Did they conform to the times?

☑ Did they break the mould?

☑ Did they follow their hearts?

☑ Did they 'do the right thing'?

☑ What words would you use to describe their relationship?

☑ Did your mother grow as a person in the relationship?

☑ Did your father grow as a person in the relationship?

☑ Did your mother feel disappointed in the relationship? If so, why?

☑ Did your father feel disappointed in the relationship? If so, why?

☑ Did your parents survive tricky times? If so, how?

☑ What did each of them think about love?

☑ What did each of them think about marriage?

☑ What did each of them think about sex?

☑ Do any of the qualities you are attracting or looking for in a partner mirror those of one of your parents? (Be honest here – sometimes we are attracted to qualities that we do not necessarily like, but which repeat something that we have experienced before.)

☑ What did your parents hope for you? What did they wish for you?

☑ **Now the dynamite question: do you agree with their messages? Think about whether you are living them out, or if there is still a voice inside you that judges potential partners according to your parents' values. Or whether you conduct relationships in a way that mirrors them.**

REVIEW

Take all this information in. Does it give you an insight into what drives you? Or into the ingredients of your attraction factor?

Now we will look at your own contribution to the mix.

What is Your Love Style?

☑ How do you approach people?

☑ In loving relationships: are you assertive, conciliatory, sensitive, logical, practical, dynamic?

☑ In working relationships: are you assertive, conciliatory, sensitive, logical, practical, dynamic?

☑ If you had to make a choice, would you rather have passion or friendship?

☑ Do you like to be independent or dependent?

REVIEW

Look at yourself from the outside, or get a friend to explain their perception of you by answering these questions on your behalf.

If You are Looking for Someone

● **What Kind of Partner?**

☑ What is on your wish list? What is your ideal?

☑ What is non-negotiable?

☑ What are you open to?

☑ What kind of relationship are you looking for: marriage, partnership, friendship?

☑ Identify the material specifics you are seeking in a prospective partner:
- Age, looks, job, income, location
- Their qualities
- Their interests
- Their likes and dislikes
- Their relationship history

☑ And then put down your own material specifics, as if you were joining a dating agency:
- Your qualities
- Your interests
- Your likes and dislikes
- Your relationship history

The Deeper Issues

☑ What do you love in life?

☑ What are you attracted to? List places, objects, types of people, ideas, vibrations.

☑ Are you attracted to difficult people?

☑ Are you attracted to people who might be considered emotionally dangerous to you?

☑ What do you imagine this partner will do for you? How will they make you feel? What impact will they have on your life?

If You are Already in a Relationship

☑ How do you feel in this person's company?

☑ Do you feel you present a better version of yourself to other people than you do to your partner? If so, in what ways?

☑ What would you change about your partner?

☑ What would you change about yourself?

☑ What do you want from your partner?

☑ What do they give you?

☑ What do they not give you?

☑ Why do you want this person in your life?

☑ What do you consider to be your main problem or issue in the relationship?

☑ What would be your cosmic order or wish for the relationship?

● **Your Relationship History**

Make a list of your significant relationships. This is not to determine the amount of time they lasted, but to reveal the impact they had on you.

List how each one started; how it made you feel; and, if this feeling changed, why it did. List what you expected out of each relationship, how it ended and what you got out of it in terms of life lessons and experience. And indicate whether you still feel you have unfinished business with this person. If you do, then move to the section on 'Letting Go of Past Relationships' (see page 134).

When to be Specific and When to Go with the Flow: The Contradiction that is Life's Mystery

If you are looking for a new relationship, it's helpful to be very clear about the kind of person you want in your life. You can, of course, write down a wish list; for example, six foot, with a six-pack, Brad Pitt lookalike, aged thirty to thirty-five, rich, unattached, successful, etc. And sometimes it's right to be specific.

Take the joke about the husband and wife, both aged sixty, whose fairy godmother told them they would each be allowed one wish. The wife asked to be sent on a cruise around the world with her darling husband, and it was granted. Then it was her husband's turn, and he asked for a woman thirty years younger than him. The fairy godmother waved her magic wand and suddenly the husband was sitting on the deck of a cruise liner, aged ninety, with his sixty-year-old wife beside him!

It's good to be specific, if only to clear out any resistance or confusion in your own head. Sometimes it's helpful to imagine yourself living out an exact cosmic order. You see it becoming real and, in some cases, will immediately realize that your 'perfect' plan has flaws, that you may in fact not want to be with the person you idealized, or it might bring up other issues. **The saying 'be careful what you wish for' is very appropriate.** You have to make sure you are ready, willing and able to live with the outcome of a dream come true.

Internet Dating and Speed Dating

Dating agencies or internet match-making sites tend to focus on the visible world rather than the invisible one. This means your key patterns, hooks and secret agenda will go unnoticed – that is until they surface on a date. Internet dating in particular has a virtual-reality quality. It can reduce people to commodities, like books or CDs. This automatically puts your mind and energy in a different dating zone. If you download somebody from the internet, and put them in your trolley, then you won't be able to pick up on their energy in the same way you would if you met them in real life.

In some cases, people meet up, are very happy with their internet date and marry one another. The internet can also get you going, if you're a receptive rather than a dynamic type and you need to start the ball rolling. But it pays to be aware that by its very nature the internet creates a different vibrational energy, which can interfere with our highly sensitive intuitive radar.

At least speed dating gives you the chance to see the person and pick up on whether you have an energy match. As in the world 'out there', it could be argued that people tend to reveal themselves in the first five minutes. It is said that if you go for an interview or view a property the key decision is made in the first five minutes, even though you might spend half an hour discussing job prospects or plumbing systems.

So, speed dating is on to something. Perhaps everything we need to know about someone is there in the five minutes we share with them before they move on to someone else. In those few moments we might be more acutely aware of what they say, how they sound and how we feel in their presence than we would if we had spent a couple of hours with them. Speed dating really gets your energy and your listening gear working acutely. **But even if you're not speed dating you should view everyone you meet as if you were.** Because, if you have all your antennae switched on, you will see that everybody reveals a lot about themselves without realizing. What are they choosing to talk about? What are they conveying with their body language? And how do they make you feel?

4

What's Your Type?

Relationship Types –
What We Draw to Us

We can use cosmic ordering to help bring a specific type of person into our lives. Alternatively, we can use it to break out of a relationship pattern. The law of resonance allows us only to attract those people that mirror our inner self. Outwardly, we may say we're looking for x, but we keep getting y, and we can't understand why we're yet again with a commitment-phobe or a control freak.

How does it happen? For a start, we're bombarded with the available, visible information about a person, which makes it harder to spot the psychological patterning that we are magnetizing. Yet, if we start looking at our pattern, identifying it, and realizing where it comes from and what it's all about, then we've got a choice about where to go with it.

Don't forget: the pattern originates with us. We are doing something to attract this type of person: giving out a particular message or inwardly believing something about ourselves that goes out into the cosmos like a heat-seeking missile. **We are giving out cosmic orders all the time without even realizing.** The trick is to become conscious of them.

We know quite confidently when someone is 'not our type', which is when they don't tick our boxes. Yet it's our inner psychological boxes that need to be explored. Our types and patterns act as magnets: at times, ironically, for the exact opposite of what we consciously want. That's when we get the chalk-and-cheese couples, who nevertheless 'go' together, and the giver-and-taker and parent-and-child types, who are busy dovetailing their roles – equally feeding off and needing one another. The committed type and the free spirit are pulling in opposite directions and are generating a magnetic attraction between each other.

Below, I will look at some of the relationship types that keep us in a specific familiar pattern. There's nothing wrong with being in that pattern if you're happy with it. But if you recognize yourself and your relationship in any of these scenarios and you would like to break free of the cycle, then you need to do something about it. Awareness makes a huge difference to cosmic ordering. Once you've truly 'got' what's happening inside you in terms of your patterns, and have become aware of what you really want, then your cosmic order will carry more power of intention.

Giver and Taker

● The Giver

The giver is the one who constantly accommodates the other person. You know that you're one if you're prepared to drop everything at the last minute in order to fit in with someone else's plans.

Givers turn up on time. They automatically think it's their job to pick up the bathroom towels, make the beds and arrive home with fresh bread for the next day. Givers always remember anniversaries, buy presents, write thank-you notes and generally make an effort to please. They are people-pleasers. But it is not that they are entirely selfless, because they get their kicks out of giving to others. In extreme cases they feel martyred, which also lends them a perverse feel-good factor. They are compelled to be the 'good person'. It is difficult to have an equal relationship with a compulsive giver, because the other person always feels they are in their debt. In some cases giving can have a secret control factor.

The Payoff

It's great to be the 'good one' in a relationship. You occupy the moral high ground, and so your partner's faults appear magnified in contrast.

What is the Pattern?

Givers are generally born into families where their own needs are not met. Hence the desire to meet other people's needs in order psychologically to break the pattern. Even though the givers get the payoff of feeling saintly, they are frequently left with the familiar feeling that their own needs have not been met. The pattern is then confirmed. They tend to attract takers because of their own need to be needed.

HOW TO IDENTIFY A GIVER

- Always available to take a phone call
- Avoids conflict
- A good listener
- Lets the other person go first
- Lets the other person do the choosing
- Tries to smooth the life and path of the other person

● The Taker

Takers possess a strong sense of entitlement. Their underlying belief is that the world and everybody in it owes them. Takers are happy to let other people pick up after them, to lie in bed while someone else makes the coffee and to use up all the hot water for themselves. They don't feel the need to remember to pass messages on to others. At the worst extreme, takers aren't even interested enough in others to ask them anything about their lives.

Conversations with takers revolve around them, and they tend to dominate the atmosphere with their opinions and moods. Everybody else is there as a backdrop to their own starring role. It never occurs to them that others might be tired, bored, hungry or have something else they want to talk about, because other people are viewed as mere satellites of the taker's all-absorbing world.

Of course takers don't verbalize this, but their psychological blueprint is narcissistic. Any arrangement is made to suit them. When a taker wants to see you, they first state their own availability and preferred venue, with an innate assumption that you will fit in with them.

The Payoff

It goes without saying. Takers' needs are usually met; they do what they want to do. They have a relationship on their own terms.

What is the Pattern?

The taker's mentality might develop from an only-child syndrome, where the child is the centre of attention and cannot ever bear to grow up. But takers can just as easily be born into larger families, where they coerce their siblings into doing what they want.

People often give in to them, because takers tend to be bullies or create such a fuss that others decide it simply isn't worth standing up to them. In fact, takers are often insecure, and deep down they do not possess a strong sense of their own centre. They only feel alive when others are showing them attention. They frequently attract givers.

HOW TO IDENTIFY A TAKER

- A 'me first' attitude
- Talks constantly about self
- Doesn't appreciate what is given
- Makes assumptions about the other person
- Has high expectations of the other person

Variations on Giver and Taker

● Leader and Follower

In the leader-and-follower relationship one person sets the pace and makes most of the decisions, while the other is prepared to give up their job or move home to be together. The follower is always playing catch-up, as the leader constantly takes off in different new directions.

● Lover and Beloved

There is always a theme of pursuit here, with the lover firing arrows of desire at the beloved. The one that is loved keeps up a game of mystery, which ensures the lover is kept interested. This type of game intrigues those who like a challenge, while being an object of desire is flattering for the ego.

The Committed and the Free Spirit

● The Committed

The committed type has a great need to settle down, feel secure and know where they stand. They are inherently loyal, never looking over your shoulder to see if someone more interesting has walked into the room. They see relationships as unfolding in progressive stages and culminating in marriage. The committed type is prepared to take on everything, including your family and any children from a previous relationship. They take on excess baggage. It goes without saying that the committed type is in the relationship for the long haul. They plan for years ahead and like to develop rituals within the relationship, which they see as cementing the bond.

The Payoff

The committed type gets to know where they stand with someone by forming a structure around the relationship. They thrive on steadiness.

What is the Pattern?

Committed types fall into two categories. One originates from a family in which the parents are glued together and the pattern is what psychologists would call 'meshed'. In other words, the family is interdependent and functions as a complete entity. So, any new relationship is expected to fit into the larger family whole. However, the other category of the committed type comes from exactly the opposite scenario. Their family of origin has disintegrated as a unit, and so they are determined to put their personal lives back together again in the form of a solid relationship. Either way, committed types are looking for someone else to commit to them to fulfil their own dream of stability.

HOW TO IDENTIFY A COMMITTED TYPE

- Talks about the relationship in positive terms
- Sees the relationship as occupying a central place in the wider context of their life
- Is available for the other person
- Isn't afraid to talk about the future
- Doesn't indulge in playing games to keep the other person dangling

---

● **The Free Spirit**

Free spirits are a law unto themselves when it comes to relationships. They are usually attracted to a wide variety of people, rather than having 'a type'. Free spirits see no problem in running relationships concurrently as they feel that no one owns them. They defy possession and justify their non-committal attitude as being an intelligent, post-modern response. They are most likely to say that they don't need a piece of paper in order to 'feel married'.

Free spirits resist convention, and are always in the process of seeing how a relationship goes rather than steering it towards a greater commitment. A fear of intimacy means that this type frequently avoids spending time just in the couple, and feels more comfortable when the primary relationship is diluted by the company of others.

The Payoff

Free spirits keep their options open, which gives them a wider pool of people to draw upon. They are unhindered by conventional ties – and even if they are in a relationship, they still remain free spirits.

What is the Pattern?

Free spirits tend to be serial daters. They can't take a relationship beyond the initial excitement stage, because once the lust and sparkle die down they are terrified of being trapped in boredom.

Commitment-phobes are often created from damage in childhood. On the surface, the family may seem very close. But often one of the parents has lionized the child and made him or her into a little prince or princess. In this case, the free-spirit personality type has been so smothered by a parent that deep down they feel they cannot be unfaithful to Mummy or Daddy.

Some free spirits come from an unconventional family, where previous generations defied convention in the settling-down stakes. Or they might have their own reasons for not wishing to repeat family patterns, and therefore protect themselves by running free.

HOW TO IDENTIFY A FREE SPIRIT

- Always talks about 'I' instead of 'We'
- Makes arrangements to do things independently, without involving the other person
- Disappears at parties and gives the impression they are available, even if they are already in a relationship
- Has a restless, highly sociable personality and likes to act spontaneously
- Dislikes routine and gets bored easily

Parent and Child

● The Parent

The parent type frequently adopts a slightly scolding, patronizing attitude towards their partner which implies that they know it all. They often earn significantly more than their partner and therefore cast themselves in the role of the person doling out the goodies. The parent is the controller, who thinks they know best. Parental types often lay down the rules of the relationship and make all the running.

The Payoff
The parent feels secure when they are in control. The imbalance in the relationship makes them feel superior.

What is the Pattern?
Often the parent type is an eldest child who is used to bossing around their siblings, or even playing parent to them. Parent types are often given responsibility from a young age and feel old beyond their years. They have a need to look after another person, but not in the same way as the giver – because the unspoken message is that the giving is strictly on the parent's terms and not on the recipient's. Sometimes the parent type is trying to redress the balance of a chaotic childhood, where they felt their own parents did not look after them enough. By creating this strong and powerful role for themselves they hope to ensure that they will never feel helpless or vulnerable.

HOW TO IDENTIFY A PARENT TYPE

- Feels happiest paying for themselves and others

- Opinionated and fixed in their ideas

- Organizes and manages holidays, social events, house purchasing

- Offers unsolicited advice

- Attached to their position or role in the world

- Takes on responsibilities

The Child

The child type doesn't want to grow up or take on responsibility in life. They see themselves as young, developing individuals, somewhat fragile and incapable of earning a decent living. They tend to get carried away with plans and dreams of the future, which often turn out to be impractical, or they lose interest in them. The child type is needy. They want others to help, support and inform them, and never to do anything for themselves if someone else can do it for them.

The child tends to get away with things because they project an image of vulnerability. Deep down the child can believe they are too special to have to deal with the ordinary mundane things of the grown-up world. They could never do a job that was 'boring', or be in a relationship that required 'hard work'.

The Payoff

The adult 'child' is often strangely attractive – particularly to the parent type, who wants to take care of them. The child is paid for, taken to places and indulged.

What is the Pattern?

Child types often come from families who never encouraged their children to grow up. Perhaps the mother smothered the child, who then played into the mother's need to be needed. When searching for a relationship the child type is unconsciously looking for a mother or father figure to replicate their early life. The child often encourages someone else to look after them by asking for advice or help, laying out their problems or saying they are 'hopeless with money'. They present themselves as either a damsel in distress, a creative, head-in-the-clouds person or as someone 'hard done by' in their relationships. They then lure their knight in shining armour or their 'yummy mummy' in to their nursery world.

HOW TO IDENTIFY A CHILD TYPE

- Happy to be paid for
- Doesn't know what they want to do
- Appears to need help/advice/support
- Lets others take control and make arrangements for them
- Doesn't have any plans for the future beyond being taken care of

The Two Halves Relationship

This kind of relationship is characterized by two people that see one another as equals, regardless of their position, income, age or experience. They are able to switch roles according to whatever is most needed at the time, because primarily they see themselves as a unit, where the good of the relationship takes precedence over their individual preferences. Although they function as two halves of a whole, each one is also perfectly able to operate as an individual in his or her own right.

5

Patterns and Blocks

How We Prevent a Cosmic Order from Being Delivered

The Denial and Defences
around Your Heart

● **The 'I Never Meet Anyone' Type**

Extraordinarily, given the x billion people milling around in the world, one of the most common phrases put about by people who are looking for a relationship is that they 'never meet anybody'. What is really happening here? Usually these people lead busy lives, hold down jobs that put them in contact with hundreds of people, have access to the internet, travel and possess huge numbers of friends.

The person who says they never meet anyone really means they are not meeting 'the one'. Actually they are coming across lots of people – none of whom is deemed 'suitable'. They may be shielding themselves from the possibility of a relationship, but denying that they are doing this. They could be cutting themselves off from opportunities of meeting the kind of person with whom they could form a happy alliance, without consciously realizing that they are doing it.

The joke about defence mechanisms is that no one thinks they've got them. They operate in secret, so we don't even realize they are there. They have a good and important job to do, but they also tend to get in the way, like bouncers at a nightclub. Obviously, we need defences to ensure our physical safety. But when it comes to our emotional lives we need to defend ourselves from anxiety. Breaking the mould and going for a big change (such as getting involved in a new relationship) can be stressful. So, not much wonder that it's far easier to keep the protective shutters down and pretend it's nothing to do with us, but that we just don't meet the right people.

However, defences need to be handled with care. They are not to be ripped away, leaving us vulnerable and exposed. We need to go gently and realize that defences serve a purpose – they keep us going; without them we imagine we will fall to pieces or our lives will be thrust into highly uncomfortable change. Of course, all this goes on inside our heads automatically. We do not consciously know we are defended. It is our invisible 'keep out' sign.

When I hear someone say, 'I never meet anybody', I envisage the person actually wearing the phrase, like a suit of armour. It is one of the best defences going. Usually there is an undercurrent of irritation accompanying the phrase, because the person often truly believes they *are* actively seeking a relationship. What I hear underneath the surface is, 'I am stuck and blocked in my quest for a soulmate, and I'm giving up and feeling hopeless about it. It's not *me*, it's *them*.' (Whoever 'they' might be, because I haven't met them!) The unspoken belief is that the soulmate is deliberately hiding from this person, evading them, despite his or her best efforts – which is why they feel angry and frustrated about it.

'I never meet anybody' is a full-stop phrase. It's a bleak statement of fact. A negative meditation. **Imagine how the universe hears it!** There is no light or optimism accompanying this thought. There is no possibility of change and no room to meet anyone. It is a mantra that is self-fulfilling.

This type of person will often have an answer for every stone that has been left unturned. The more suggestions you make, the more the note of irritation creeps into their voice. 'I have tried that,' they might exclaim, or give some other reason why they can't make the salsa class, or say they believe that someone younger than them would never be interested. Even if they hear about amazing relationships happening to other people they quickly say, 'That would never happen to me.'

Scratch the surface of the 'not meeting anybody' type and you will quickly see that they are hugely invested in things remaining the same. Staying in the groove. Although, of course, this is buried so deep that if someone dared to point it out they would be hurt, defensive and angry – with that very person.

The more these difficult feelings churn around inside somebody, the more they leak out on the surface. You might believe that you are open to meeting somebody and are just waiting to find Mr or Miss Right. And you might go through the motions of turning up at events, making an effort to look good, chatting to people, but the 'I never meet anybody' part of you is actually running the show. You need to replace this mantra with a more positive one.

In order to move on, the part of you that doesn't want to break the pattern needs to be neutralized. Awareness is everything – you need to be clear about what you want to do.

You can start by listening to yourself saying that you never meet anybody – catch yourself out. That's the first step towards reprogramming yourself. The resigned air that accompanies the statement speaks of a long, deeply ingrained problem. 'I never meet anybody' is an angry but wistful longing for contact, a fear of rejection, and a fear that the world/universe is a bad place that doesn't meet your needs. That the person ('my Mr/Miss Right') is withholding him/herself from you – and that's before you've even met! The phrase speaks volumes about your pattern. Everything is contained within it. Your impatience, frustration and fear is present in the room as you confide in a friend, who feels the tension as you speak – and perceives the terribleness of it. It can prompt a reaction in them – the urge to make it better – which, inevitably, is met with a rebuff.

The 'I never meet anybody' type thinks of the universe as a withholding parent, and of themselves as the child, powerless to alter the status quo. At the same time they wonder what they are doing wrong. They might be making a great effort to do all the right things, but their own inner image/perception of themselves as a child in the face of an unfair/controlling/denying universe is blocking anything new from happening.

● Saying It But Not Believing It

You need to become aware of your own resistance. For those who say, 'I want to meet someone' – ask why it doesn't happen. Ask yourself what is stopping/preventing it.

Your Hidden Agenda

You might believe yourself to be an open person, simply wanting to meet someone. However, although you say 'someone', it's not just anyone. It's Mr or Miss Right, who looks like x, earns y and has the qualities of z. It's always the specifics that stand in the way. If you are looking for your dream partner, that is precisely what it will remain – a dream. You need to look for your *real* partner.

Unconsciously, some people are looking for a powerful, wealthy partner who they believe will take away their insecurity. For instance, they are only attracted to alpha males and, even though they may have had some disappointing experiences with them, this remains their unconscious blueprint. There is nothing wrong with seeking a highly successful mate. However, because success is what drives the alpha male, he often has less quality time to give to other areas, which means he is often emotionally unavailable.

You might come from a family where your parents have such a wonderful marriage that it's a hard act to follow. Conversely, you might only be attracted to those who let you down or fail to commit, because it mirrors something in your parents' relationship.

> Being aware of your own hidden agenda is key. Realizing that you have concealed expectations and that these are keeping you stuck is a crucial component of what will make cosmic ordering work for you.

Is it an unfair world out there? Yes. We don't always get what we want. But we also have a part to play in creating the unfairness and in generating our own patterns. Our resistance comes through because something within us is saying, 'No, this is too scary.' You are creating your own impasse. You think you can't do something, or you're actually stopping it from happening. You are caught in a strange bind, where the more you want it, the more the counterforce comes in.

So You Want a Relationship – Is Resistance Stopping You?

What is Resistance?

It is whatever stops or blocks us from within. Resistance reveals a fear of letting ourselves go into the unknown.

How do you know when it's operating? Whenever you feel powerless or stuck – this is a great clue that resistance is going on. When you have a problem, there is usually an equal part of yourself that doesn't want to find the solution.

What are the other symptoms of resistance? Feeling blank about what you can do or confused as to what your next step should be. The mental fog is something you create so that you don't have to make a decision.

Why do we stay stuck? There is usually a hidden payoff in remaining stuck. It feels safer to stay where you are, even though you want the change. Resistance performs an important role in looking after us. It shuts out difficult problems and protects us from the very things that scare us. If we talk about wanting a relationship, but have a fear of intimacy deep down, then resistance will pop up and keep us away from the perceived threat. It's a really invisible business and you have to be prepared to be very honest with yourself in order to see it. Hardly anyone will actually own up to a fear of intimacy. We can't even admit it to ourselves. If we don't want to see, acknowledge or look at it then it will go underground and become the driving force of a resistance that is our counterforce to meeting someone.

The natural instinct might be to fight the resistance. To try to cut it out, remove it in one fell swoop. But that would expose us too much. It is not as simple as that, and we need to acknowledge the need for protection. The first step is actually to embrace the resistance: to allow it, acknowledge it and know why it's there. To realize that it is useful in some ways, but at the same time is keeping us stuck. We can't just say, 'Now I will simply stop being resistant.'

We have to see how it comes into play, what kind of situations make it active. To see where our buttons are being pressed and resistance rushes in to defend us from danger. We may be yearning for a relationship but it is simply too dangerous for us to enter into that emotional, intimate territory.

Defences

● The Stories We Tell Ourselves

The more fragile we are, then the more defences we need, because the world doesn't feel safe to us. We carry around this emotional insurance policy, but it costs a lot. In fact it takes a lot out of us to keep it going. We have to keep investing in our defence patterns, to keep feeding ourselves the same story. One client kept telling me, 'There are no men out there' – this was her denial and her defence; it became *her* truth, even though it was not the truth and it didn't reflect her hopes. I asked her, 'What would happen if there were?'

At the same time you are telling yourself (and anyone else who will listen) the same story over and over again, you are running another possible storyline which you also tell yourself and the world – that you really *want* to meet somebody. It is energy fighting energy. You are doing this to yourself. You long for something and then resist it, don't believe in it, run away from it or sabotage it.

Some of the stories we tell ourselves are guaranteed to keep us narrow and limited. We can call these 'rackets' – we keep the racket going and we kid ourselves that the reason we can't do *x*, *y* or *z* is because we don't have the money, the time or the opportunity. We are being dishonest with ourselves, as it boils down to our own fear of change. We won't take the risk.

We all tend to occupy familiar territory in life. We go to the same places, do the same things, hang out with the same people – and we inhabit the same emotional territory too. It feels safe; we know what to expect. And we cut ourselves off from letting anything new happen. In ancient times the world was believed to be square, with definite edges that were dangerous. Legend has it that maps were once drawn with 'here be dragons' written in the outside margin, indicating the unknown. Of course, we now know the world is round and that we won't fall over the edge, but we still create our own imaginary boundaries, or edges, where we simply won't go – either physically or psychologically.

We are so invested in the myth of who we are that we close ourselves off to our potential. We form our identities around our work, how old we are and what we've got – and they become set in stone. The more we believe in these superficial indications of who we are, the less likely we are to feel truly free. It becomes more difficult to act spontaneously; we turn down invitations because we think we won't enjoy the experience. We become denser in our thinking patterns and more emotionally blocked, as we carry around all these roles, identities and expectations. We expend all of our energy in holding on to what we've got and who we are. **But the truth is that we could reinvent ourselves if we wanted to.** It's very important to remember that we always have a choice – and yet so easy to forget.

How Much Freedom Do We Really Have?

The answer to this question, within the free world, is as much as you want or as much as you think you have. We actually live in a void that we fill by creating our own personal comfort zones. And once we have stepped into our comfort zone, life continues to send us our delivery every week and we don't think to change it. So many things are pulled in towards us by our existing patterns and mindset. We attract them in, and then wonder why we always end up with the same order!

The real promise offered by cosmic ordering is that you stop closing yourself down and you open yourself up to possibilities.

Questions to Ask Yourself about Your Story

☑ What is my story/my pattern around relationships?

☑ How did it come into being? Think about your childhood story, your parents' relationship.

☑ How do I keep myself stuck and blocked?

☑ How would I like things to be?

☑ Am I truly willing to rewrite the script?

Write down anything relevant – any insight into your story.

6
The Hard-Work Miracle

How to Make Cosmic Ordering
Work for You ...

So, now you are aware of your wish list. In theory, you've ticked your boxes. And you've looked at some of the things that might be standing in the way, such as defences, patterns and your story.

Now it's time to go one stage further. This chapter will give you specific techniques to work through anything that might be preventing the cosmic order from manifesting itself. You will be working on yourself here: questioning, analysing, visualizing and meditating.

Cosmic ordering is a combination of miracles and hard work!

Getting closer to your dream happens in little moments, through small choices – we need to dare to be different. And sometimes a slight change can make a really big impression and be very encouraging.

However, we shouldn't expect to shift a huge pattern of resistance overnight. The universe can't deliver your order through a heavy field of defence or denial. It just isn't possible. You need to clear your energy field so that the universe can help you to get what you want.

That means doing some work on yourself: some assessment and appraisal. If you don't feel able to answer the questions below by yourself, then get someone you trust to answer them on your behalf. This can be a very interesting exercise, as the other person will often be able to see straight through your defences and into the heart of the matter.

Do some visualizations and meditations, and then activate your will by taking your next step. Keep going. Stay motivated. Don't give up on yourself – or on the universe.

... Even If Nothing's Ever Worked So Far

Your next step is to focus on where you are stuck and how to change your position.

Remember, *You* are the One Who Creates Your Reality

Here are some questions to ask yourself:

- What is it that I really want?

- Why do I want it?

- What is stopping me from having it?

  a) The universe isn't delivering

  b) I'm not sure if it's possible

  c) I'm trying everything, but nothing happens

  d) I'm afraid that if I had it I wouldn't be up to it

  e) I'm worried about change or the unknown

  f) I am protecting myself

  g) I don't know (which is your resistance in operation)

  h) Another reason

- What is my payoff in remaining stuck, in not having this order delivered? Am I getting anything out of life by staying the same?

- What would my life look like and how would I feel if I carried on like this for ever?

- Do I have times when I feel I'm moving forward? If so, when? In what circumstances? What happens to block it again?

- How did I get into this situation? List events, attitudes and people that have contributed to this present problem. What did they do? What did I do?

- Do I believe it is possible for the situation to change?

- Is it possible for *me* to change?

- What am I hoping for?

- What do I wish the outcome to be?

Visualize your block as a brick that is made up of all the insights you have gleaned from your response to these questions. Now lay it down as the foundation stone of your cosmic order. You will build up from here.

Techniques to Keep
Your Energy Flowing

Now you need some techniques, in case you become stuck, to get the energy moving again so you can start to make things happen. Remember, you may not be able to enforce a change, but you *can* free up the energy and get it moving again.

Being able to attract what it is you desire requires you to work on your ability to pull things towards you. Being able to manifest what you want on the physical plane is an art which can be perfected. In order to pull things out of the air, you need to develop greater magnetism.

Firstly, stating the obvious, you need to place your cosmic order in whatever way you wish.

1 *Write down your cosmic order and place it with the powers that be.* Put it on your fridge where you constantly see it.

2 *Ask yourself what the next three steps would be to get things moving for you.* Write them down. Make them achievable, manageable and possible within a short time frame.

3 *Tell a mentor* what you're about to do and get them to check in with you to see if you're still on the case.

4 *Acting as if ... the realistic fantasy.* Now imagine that you are living life without this problem. Or that your cosmic order has already been delivered.

- If you were free of your problem what would *your life* be like?
- If you were free of your problem what would *you* be like?
- How would you act and how would you be?
- Get in touch with how you would feel if your cosmic order had already been delivered. Amplify this emotion, feel it in your body, in your mind and in all of your being. To be able to experience this, to imagine having your desire and living it out, is really important.
- When you have got hold of this feeling, write down any words that describe it. What is it? Do you know anyone else who lives like this or who embodies this feeling? Could you take a leaf out of their book?

Your mission now is to *act as if* this fantasy has already become reality. Act as if this cosmic order has been delivered into your life, you're living it out, you are it. Even if what you wanted to happen hasn't happened, just act as if it has. Whenever and wherever you can. If you create a separation between yourself and your wish then it becomes harder for it to manifest itself. You must *be* whatever your wish is, connect with it, become it, or *act as if* you are aligning yourself with it. If you see your wish as obtainable, it's a crucial factor in getting closer to its deliverance.

This technique subtly alters your attraction pattern. It works on the premise that 'like attracts like' and you become able to magnetize the people and situations that you are wanting.

Another effective technique to increase your power of pulling things towards you and to give you more leverage in life is 'the magnet meditation'. This great little exercise can be used to shore up your resources of self-esteem and make you feel more positive and confident about getting what you want – any time, any place, anywhere.

5   *The magnet meditation.* Imagine you are a magnet. Picture yourself as being infused with magnetic energy that attracts whatever you want. Imagine your desires coming towards you simply because they are being pulled in your direction. Become aware of how easily life works when you have this

magnetic energy. How simple it is to get what you want. But there is a caveat: be careful what you wish for. The magnet meditation is very powerful and you need to know that you're attracting the right things rather than all kinds of lumps and bits that you thought you wanted, but which are really just excess baggage.

If you are still wrestling with issues that are bringing you down, then try the following higher-perspective meditation.

Gaining a Higher Perspective on the Problem

Find somewhere comfortable and quiet, where you won't be interrupted, and sit with your back straight. Close your eyes and breathe deeply. Let go of any tension in your body, feel it leaving you.

Now visualize yourself sitting as you are on the chair. Mentally look down on yourself sitting in the room and become aware that you are meditating on a particular issue in your life. See the room vividly in your mind, with its furniture and colours. Imagine looking down on the house or building from above, with you inside it, holding this issue. Now imagine you are seeing it all from even higher up; you can see the street, the village or the town, and everyone going about their day-to-day business, while you are sitting inside on a chair, in a room, in your house. Now go higher still and see the country you are living in, and see the whole world with all its countries and people. Send light from this position down to yourself, as if you are sitting under a spotlight.

Visualize yourself with this problem and run through the patterns and events that have led up to it, as if rewinding a film. Only the relevant bits will be shown to you. Is there a thread you can see? Is there anything you can see from up here that you didn't know about down there? Are there any words, inspirations, feelings or advice you can send down to yourself from your higher point of awareness?

Slowly come back down to earth, become aware of the world, your own country, your own town, your own street, your own house, the room you are in, the chair you are sitting on. Wriggle your toes and hands, open your eyes and come back. Write down what you have experienced, how you felt and any help you may have gained.

If you find it difficult to believe and trust that your wish will be granted, or you find it hard to stop trying to control everything, then try the following technique.

● Technique for Going with the Flow

Allow yourself to drop into a meditative, contemplative state. Feel the relaxation in your body where all effort has dropped away. Imagine you are looking at a river that will take you where you want to go. All you have to do is to get in (this is safe water, not rapids) and float along, allowing its gentle current to carry you to your final destination. The river may meander, but that is fine. You have enough time. You don't need to worry about the journey, or steer, or make anything happen. Flow along with the river. Experience what it feels like to place your trust in something else. Let go of any desire to control, just watch the scenery, enjoy the experience and know that you *will* arrive at a place that is right for you.

This technique is useful to repeat whenever you are getting stressed about the whys, hows and wherefores of life.

If you can't get a handle on what to do next, try the following technique.

● The Choice Meditation

Imagine you are walking along the path of your life. Then you come to a fork in the road. You have to make a choice. Imagine you have a map and can see where each road leads. Look at what the map is telling you about these two choices. Is one a faster route than the other? Is one more beautiful? Will one get you to your destination in a far simpler way? Will the other involve the possibility of getting lost? Do both roads lead to the same place, so whichever one you take will be okay? Or are you about to go in a very different direction? Get a feeling before making this choice. It is important. Realize that you are free to move whichever way you want in your journey through life.

All of these exercises and techniques will help to increase your *power of attainment*. But there is one ingredient that is essential to your skill in cosmic ordering. **It is the power of intention.**

What is the Difference between Intention and Desire?

We need to turn up the volume of intention if cosmic ordering is to work for us. Having an intention is very different to having a desire, and in the process of cosmic ordering **intention is everything**.

What exactly is *intention* as opposed to *desire*? Intention is a conscious state. It implies purpose, taking responsibility for what happens and actively engaging with getting something done. For example, if you intend to lose weight, then it is likely you will go on a diet, take more exercise, set goals and do everything in your power to break bad habits. Desire, on the other hand, is defined as 'an unsatisfied longing'. It is a passive state. So if you only desire to lose weight, then you may want to drop some pounds or *wish* it would happen, but it's not going to unless you *do* something.

If we come from a place of intention then things start to pull together. They become connected. However, if we come from a place of desire then we experience fragmentation, where all our desires are competing with one another. We can get lost in this realm; sometimes our desires are in so much conflict that we even lose sight of what it is that we really want. If we are driven by our desires they can be so powerful that they feel compulsive. And the unfortunate thing is that even if we do fulfil them, they are rarely satisfying for long. Once we have achieved our desire then we are pulled towards having more of it, or to reaching out for the next one. Whatever it was we wanted, when we eventually get it we realize that it still isn't enough for us. We're in a cycle that keeps us on a hamster's wheel.

It may seem as if desire makes the world go round – corporations thrive on it; advertising promotes it; and we chase around after this or that, thinking it will make us happy. Yet when our energy is scattered we are less effective. In the pursuit of desire we sometimes waste our essence, our substance, our vital life force. It's important not to identify with desires too much – they are what carry us away, often into old habits.

But feeling desire is not all bad. It can be a positive thing, because desire puts us in touch with what we want. It can be the trigger to shake us out of our inertia. It can be good to desire something and to want an outcome – but it's best not to get too attached or stuck in a mindset about how it can be delivered. By its very nature attachment is intense. When it is operating, we have to have whatever it is we are wanting. We feel our lives depend upon it.

According to Buddhist theory, desire and attachment are major sources of unhappiness. The Dalai Lama talks of 'a non-needful beingness', which doesn't grasp or cling either to objects, situations or people. You might think that cosmic ordering goes against this principle, as 'ordering' implies that we want something. We do. But the skill in cosmic ordering hinges on our ability to intend something to happen, without feeling compulsive about it.

You can step off your hamster's wheel of attachment by cultivating intention. Intention is more purposeful and mindful than desire. With intention you can experience maximum energy with minimum effort.

Using intention means you are operating from a greater level of self-awareness. *You choose to do something, rather than have to.* By using intention you can meet your needs rather than your wants.

Do You Make Your Own Luck?

THINK LUCKY!

Research has shown that if you think of yourself as lucky then you attract more opportunities.

Sometimes it seems as though the exponents of cosmic ordering make it sound so easy, as if you can get everything you want simply by asking for it. Then all you need to do is lie back and wait for it to come knocking on your door. But I don't believe it really does work like that. Particularly if you have any patterns of resistance that will make it harder for new possibilities to come through.

KEY WAYS TO GET LUCKY

This is how you make your own luck and, as someone once said, 'I had to work very hard to get this lucky!'

- It's not enough just to *want* something to happen, you have to be prepared to *do* something about it too. The universe expects you to do your bit. Making an effort is also a key ingredient. You attract opportunities by knowing how to use them, just as energy follows energy. You will need to start developing the attitude and the intention to make clear choices and firm decisions to head in a chosen direction.

- If you've been trying everything, but feel as though you're knocking your head against a brick wall, you might need to **trust the process** more so that cosmic ordering can work for you. It is not about being in control and having everything you want, but about trusting and letting go, so that the universe can get through. You might need to develop a willingness to surrender to a flow of energy that will get you where you want to go.

- But here is the paradox behind creating luck: be 100 per cent behind it, but do not allow yourself to get attached to the outcome. And don't get attached to how it has to happen. The minute you start boxing yourself in with elaborate detail about how you want things to be, then the delivery system gets blocked. The technique of being committed to an event happening, without trying to control it, requires some patience and practice. But once you've got it, luck will follow.

Are You a Receptive or Dynamic Energy Type?

This brings us back to the theme of fate or free will. To what extent can we affect the outcome? People tend to fall into two types: the more receptive type feels that there is a larger design, and allows life to unfold accordingly; while the dynamic type believes we create our own destiny and that with a strong sense of purpose we can get what we want.

Receptive qualities are opposite to dynamic qualities:

RECEPTIVE	DYNAMIC
Yin	Yang
Love	Will
Flow	Action
'The Grand Design'	Free Will
Passive	Aggressive
Intuitive	Logical
Being	Doing

People tend either to be one type or the other. If you want to improve your cosmic ordering hit-rate then it's important to establish which one you are at the start, so that you can work towards bringing the opposite type's qualities into your life.

Receptive Types

You are a receptive type if you:

- see connections very easily

- have a tendency to go with the flow

- are fluid and prefer 'being' to 'doing'

- believe everything will work out in the end, that it will be okay and you just have to trust the process

- hand the outcome over to fate and say that everything is meant to be

Your issue: you see the potential and the possibilities, but have difficulty in making it real. You lose your way and have no focus.

Dynamic types

You are a dynamic type if you:

- believe you are responsible for what happens

- believe you can make things happen

- enjoy challenging yourself and tackling problems

- feel that solutions come out of making choices

- like to be in control and know what you're doing at all times

Your issue: you do everything you can to make things happen, but have difficulty in trusting the universe. You like to be in control and can't hand the delivery over to the cosmos.

In order for cosmic ordering to work you need to use the qualities of both receiving and acquiring.

If you identify with being *receptive* then you need to become much more active and dynamic in pursuit of your wishes. You need to take practical steps and challenge yourself to make your dreams become reality. Spend more time getting out there into the world and stepping into the unknown, rather than sitting back and waiting for things to come to you in the fullness of time.

If, however, you identify with being more *dynamic*, then you need to work regularly on the visualization techniques above, especially those that help you go with the flow. You need to steel yourself to let go more often and learn how 'to just be'. Remember that you can get what you want simply by staying still rather than chasing after it. The ability to receive is an art which requires a certain level of openness. You need to feel comfortable about receiving.

How Will You Know
When the Time is Right?

Any change requires an ending and a new beginning. You might be changing something small, like a habit, or you might be tackling a recurring pattern or, in some cases, you might want a radical change that calls for you to give up your old life as you know it.

Any change requires intention, energy and an act of will so that you can move away from the past and choose to do things differently. If you're trying to change a familiar pattern you need to tell yourself, 'I'm not going down that road this time.' You need to make an effort. You really have to want to change at a deeper level, rather than just thinking it would be nice if it happened. You need to engage the will.

Sometimes you have to let go of something first to allow you to do what you want to do. Letting go is not just a thought process, but a true relinquishment or inner full-stop that happens at a pivotal time of your life, and continues to manifest itself ever after. Being willing implies openness. To go for something new means you have to be ready to do what's right for you and become aware of self-limiting patterns.

● ● ●

You know when the time is right. It's when you arrive at a moment of readiness to try something out. This is where Jung's theory of *synchronicity* comes into play. Whatever it is you have in your mind will attract similar energy. For instance, you want to go to a certain place and you bump into somebody who has just come back from there. Or you have an idea and then pick up a book which tells you more about it. Little signals and messages start resonating with what you're trying to do. These are the signposts that say, 'Yes, it's the right time for your wish to fall into place.'

You then need a flexible outline of how you want things to be. I say flexible, because you are not totally in control. *You are willing for things to change, and you are open to whatever comes along.*

7

Desire and Expectation

How Cosmic Ordering
Can Help a Relationship

● **You are with Someone and It isn't Working**

You can use cosmic ordering when a good relationship is going off the rails. Sometimes you might get stuck in a cycle of blips and could use a bit of cosmic ordering to help pull you out of it. It can connect you to the bigger picture. When you are caught in a problem you can step outside of your particular issue and see that the relationship is teaching you something about yourself. You can ask the universe for guidance on what it is you are meant to be learning from the problem. You can request for help in letting go of bad feelings and in becoming more accepting.

● **When We Feel Compelled to be with Someone**

If you're in the grip of a compulsion to be with someone

then you're in a spin-cycle, where the universe cannot communicate with you. This is when you feel lost. Lost in an addiction to a person. You want to be with someone, you desire certain things out of the relationship, you expect the person to behave a certain way – you place so much importance on the relationship that it only leads to your feeling let down.

Sometimes it isn't possible to have the person that we want in our lives. They are otherwise engaged, not 'right for us' or simply unavailable. We can waste a lot of time in attempting to control the situation: trying both to make it happen and to force the other person into doing what we want. But the universe is always available to us as a means of letting go of an attachment that will not work for us. If we can learn to go with the flow then the universe can take us beyond the limitations of that attachment. And so we can become open to something or someone else.

How Cosmic Ordering Can Improve Reactive Relationships

You might be in a relationship that feels like a cosmic joke rather than a match made in heaven. At this point, it's easy to lose sight of your connection to the universe.

If you are stuck in a *reactive* relationship then you can't read the signals, find any meaning, get a perspective or move forward.

First of all you need to look at your relationship. Is it reactive? In other words, does it constantly press the buttons that make you jump into repeat patterns of conflict, without being able to stop yourself? The cosmos can't break the cycle for you. But if you are ready to stop playing this game with the other person then you can move up a gear and ask the cosmos for help in making your experience together a happier one.

SYMPTOMS OF A REACTIVE RELATIONSHIP

- Are you caught in an ongoing pattern of conflict?
- Are you constantly dealing with scuffles that take you straight back to the main recurring argument?
- Do you try to micro-manage your partner, so that conflict can be avoided, but find you still fall into the trap?
- Do you feel as though you are simply surviving in the relationship rather than enjoying it?
- Have your friends and family advised you to walk away, but you are so hooked that this feels impossible?

When two people are connected on a higher level, they are able to realize their potential of being, having and doing, rather than conducting a relationship based on loss and lack, where each is defended against the other, the enemy.

You might think your partner's attitude will prevent any change. But it only takes one of you to change. You don't have to both be at the same level.

The kind of relationship indicated above is based on a win/lose energy. It is very black and white, with no shades of grey, and it revolves around who is right and who is wrong. The more highly charged the relationship becomes, the more adrenaline is generated between the two of you, and the more caught up in the problem you become.

The relationship is also about possession – where one of you wants either to possess or to be possessed. It is based on the fear that you might run out of time or lose love. When a relationship has these fears at its core, then it's difficult to find any peace with the other person. Fear creates a see-saw of emotions, a pounding of adrenaline, and it prevents us from creating a quality contact. The feeling that you have to hang on to that person at all costs is in itself quite a cost. It deprives you of the ability to open up. Clinging to someone is a manifestation of closing down. You are caught in a negative cycle of energy in which the universe cannot reach you.

● The Battle of Win/Lose and How the Cosmos Can't Get Through

When your relationship is based on a constant diet of fireworks, the adrenaline this produces becomes addictive. You think you are obsessed with the person but, in fact, you are addicted to the excitement of the adrenaline rush, which gives you a buzz and is similar to the rush of the 'in love' feeling. This person and the dynamic of the relationship triggers a real high. The problem is that it's followed by a real low.

You can become so intoxicated by the ups and downs of the relationship that it's difficult to go cold turkey, which is the only way you will get a balanced perspective. We mistake the drama for love, because it feels so heightened, so passionate. If we are not careful we can convince ourselves it is 'so right'.

The reality is that the relationship is very depleting, and our obsession with this person and with *winning* the relationship prevents us from standing back and seeing it as it really is. We cut ourselves off from the cosmos and fail to read the signals. The result is that emotionally we become out of balance and we damage our well-being by living in a state of constant tension.

THE TOXIC BLOCKS TO RELATING

Do we have any power over what happens in our relationships? We always do, although sometimes we may need to reclaim it.

Does the universe send us the kind of people who can teach us a thing or two? Yes. We imagine things should be perfect between us and our partner, but usually we learn the most from our difficult relationships. These are the ones that require some work on our part.

Sometimes, however, we get so caught up in our toxic blocks that the relationship gets well and truly stuck. That's when we need to dig deep inside ourselves to discover why we are in this trap.

● The Cinderella Complex

This is a very common trap. It means we are dependent on another person to feel good about ourselves, and we only see ourselves as we are reflected in their eyes. This is dangerous because it means we are not building up a strong inner core, we have low self-esteem and we lack the ability to feel okay, either with or without the other person.

In some cases, you might project your destiny on to someone else, so that seemingly they then have the power to determine the outcome of your life. You remain small, and your life is permanently on hold as you wait for *them* to make all the decisions. To decide if they are going to commit, for instance.

Letting go of the image of yourself as Cinderella can be surprisingly hard. The fairy-tale dynamic will have to come to an end, and the illusion to be dealt with, as you try to meet life on more realistic terms. Dropping the part of Cinderella means taking responsibility for your own life and realizing that you might be able to do something about what's going on. That you can't just blame others.

One very important component of cosmic ordering is that **we can only create our own reality when there is no one else to blame!** In other words, if we feel that somebody else is to blame for our situation, then we are powerless – because they are the one that is in control, and so we automatically lose any power to change anything. The moment we stop blaming others then we gain the freedom to create something better.

The Game of Ping-Pong

There you are in your relationship, with the arguments flying back and forth. There is one level where this is healthy and another where it is toxic. You will instinctively know the difference between them. The toxic argument is ongoing and it can be triggered by small things, but it quickly gets deep beneath your skin. It is characterized by a simmering resentment and a continual battle which both people in the relationship are struggling to win.

It always takes two people to create a problem. There is some kind of unconscious pact to play a game that keeps the issue going on and on, both parties batting it between them like a well-rehearsed game of ping-pong. It is self-perpetuating, yet **it only takes one person to change it**.

To make the change happen you need to step outside of the known parameters and stop the destructive behaviour or dynamic. You have to approach this with a genuine willingness to do things differently, and not be half-hearted. You might think you don't play games, but you do. This ongoing battle/pattern/conflict is, in fact, a game. And if there is going to be any change then you need to take responsibility for your own part in it. What is it you do to keep it going?

With such an ingrained pattern between the two of you, you have to do more than just dream or desire that things were different. You need to muster up every ounce of motivation and *be willing for it to be different*. But it's so easy to slip back into the game of ping-pong, because it feels familiar and it gives you the payoff of feeling that you are right and they are wrong.

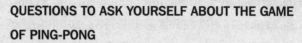

QUESTIONS TO ASK YOURSELF ABOUT THE GAME OF PING-PONG

- How am I keeping it going?
- Do I think of somebody in a particular way, and then find they conform to my view of them?
- Am I willing to let go of the conflict I have with this person?
- What do I get out of the game? (Being right; enjoying the drama; venting my stress; enjoying the challenge?)
- Can I let go of the idea that I want something from this person?
- What is the conflict really about for me?
- Do I have the desire, belief and expectancy that things can change?

Review the Game and Your Mindset

If we think of someone in a certain way then they will *be* that way – for us. Obviously they are not always going to be the same, as other people will have different views of them and will experience them from different angles. Yet we are continually keeping people stuck by seeing them through our own personal lens. We box them in. *However, it's true to say that we can change the world by changing our perception.*

If we accept somebody as they are, without wanting to change them, then we are creating the possibility of something new happening. You might think the other person will never change, because they are so stuck. But if you hold the possibility for change then you have more scope.

The game of ping-pong is often triggered by arguments that start over something relatively small. There is so much that overlays the real and deeper issue that we think we're arguing about *x*, when really it's *y* that's the problem. There's a reality behind the reality. Recognizing what it is this person is triggering within you is a vital step towards dealing with it.

Wanting to Clear the
Emotional Issues

You need to become aware of what it is you're holding on to, i.e. blame, guilt, resentment. You are the one who is suffering as a result of harbouring these feelings. They attach themselves to your emotional body and clog up your psyche, creating a heavy, impenetrable and, in some cases, bitter feeling. Letting go of this will loosen up your entire energy. But you can't just pay lip service to the idea of being free of it – you really have to *want* to clear it up.

> You can ask the universe to help you become free of these feelings. But don't ask it to change the other person, because it is not the remit of the universe to do so.

If you have high self-esteem you are automatically less threatened by whatever anyone else says. You can cultivate this. You can begin by thinking, 'No matter what you say, I'm not going to feel threatened.' As Eleanor Roosevelt once observed, 'No one can make me feel inferior without my consent.'

You can ask the universe for help in feeling better about yourself, and in letting go of any of those 'not good enough' messages that may lurk inside you.

How Can the Universe Help?

Can we look beyond the behaviour of the other person and what is happening between the two of us? In some instances, it helps to improve our connection if we see this person as a soul with a personality. Rather than seeing them as someone who is behaving badly or not doing what we want, we can see beyond or deep inside it. We can achieve this by realizing that there is more to the other person than being a walking argument waiting to happen! If you expand your awareness of what constitutes a person, taking into account all their neuroses, fears, attachments, insecurities, needs, desires and wants, then you create a realm where a deeper connection can happen. If we could just stop wanting to wipe out the part of their personality we don't like, but rather include it (without judgement if possible), this means we can move on, even if we remain in the relationship.

We don't have to like or agree with what they say or do, but it helps if we can accept them as a person. You can ask the universe for help with this acceptance – because although you may not be able to change this person, you can change yourself.

Technique for Seeing Deep Inside the Issue

The next exercise will help you to see deep inside the pattern and into the other person. It should be revealing.

Place two chairs opposite each other, with a cushion on the floor in between. One will be your chair and one will represent the other person's. Sit in your own chair and visualize the other person sitting opposite you. Recall the tension that exists between you. Perhaps you don't feel comfortable with this person, or they irritate you, or the difficulties between you prevent you from feeling generous towards them. If it helps, write down what the difficulty is from your point of view, explaining how you feel about it.

Now switch chairs! Visualize yourself as the other person. Try to imagine what it's like to be them: what you look like to them, how you present yourself and how you feel. Exaggerate. Make some statements that they might make: I am *x*, I feel *x*, I think *x*, I defend myself by *x*. Become them as you look at yourself in the other chair, and notice what they see and how they feel about you. Now imagine having their dreams, hopes and fears. Really take them on board. What are they about? How do they make you behave? Write down any insights if you wish.

Now become neutral by dissociating yourself from either person and from the problem. Sit on the cushion in between the two chairs. Are you able to see from here anything more about this issue or the deeper needs of the two people involved? Have you any awareness of what drives them, and what needs to happen for a pattern to be broken or a better understanding to emerge? Write down any insights.

Doing this helps us to see our *projections*. All along, we have looked at the other person through our own distorted lens. By *becoming them* we might realize how it actually feels to *be them*. Projection is something we all do, most of the time, because it is so difficult to be transparent and to see others clearly. We make personal judgements, comments and decisions about other people which are based on our own values. We even view them as people who behave in a way that we would 'never do'. Yet this is because we have repressed an aspect of ourselves that is still lurking in the undergrowth of our psyche. Any time that we get a charge of energy around a particular person, it's a signal that something about them is connecting to something in *us*.

Stop Playing the Game

We can choose how we respond to others. We could choose to remain serene and have a handle on things, if that is what we wish.

You can practise responding, rather than reacting, by:

- taking the time to allow a plan, an idea or a response to come together slowly
- breaking a habit
- taking a risk and doing something that is outside your comfort zone

Start implementing these tools in your relationship.

Letting Go of Past Relationships

We can continue our attachment to somebody long after the relationship is technically over. We carry a torch for someone, we compare other people to them, we become nostalgic for the good times we had together. Or we continually replay the bad times in our minds, thereby maintaining the history in the present. The person is a ghostlike presence in our lives, and so much of our emotional psychic energy is stuck to them that there is little available for anybody new.

Tackling your unfinished business is vital (even if you do it on your own). Ask yourself:

- What is it that you can't let go of?
- What are you holding on to?
- How does this prevent you from getting on with the rest of your life?
- Do you still long for this person? Why?
- Is this the only person in the world with the quality you long for?
- What didn't you say to them?
- What didn't you do?

- What prevents you from resolving this?
- Can you accept and allow this relationship to be finished, and to achieve a state of peace within yourself?

All you have to do is to work on your own bit of unfinished business.

Technique for Letting Go of Someone

Imagine you are standing in one half of a figure of eight. The person you are trying to let go of is standing in the other half. You are joined together, but separate. Place anything that belongs to you within your own circle and anything that belongs to them in theirs, including words, events, possessions and experiences. Gradually you can see the two circles moving away from one another, separating into two complete and individual units.

8

It's Up to You

One of the most exciting aspects of cosmic ordering is that so much of life really is up to you. Okay, things will happen that you didn't wish for, fate decrees that certain elements come into your life, but after that **it's up to you!** You are free to do whatever you want with life. We make of it what we will. We can choose to go on playing with opportunities, engaging with life, putting out some cosmic orders and staying positive.

The Key Ingredients

● What are You Looking For?

First up, it's very important to become conscious of what exactly you are looking for. Don't be vague. Stop letting the old patterns play out in your life. Start actively looking instead of day-dreaming.

● Can You Trust?

Check out how cynical you are. Do you believe in the power of cosmic ordering? Can you place your trust in something higher, in some kind of divine wisdom, guidance and meaning? Being able to look the cosmos in the eye and have the nerve to place an order requires faith in life. Faith isn't automatic. If you work on developing your intuition, and if you believe in the wisdom and meaning of life, then you are forming a connection with the unseen. It means letting go of any sceptical attitude and protecting yourself from other people's cynicism. It's so easy to doubt, to mock. *It's so easy to close down. But closing down won't get you anywhere*. It will just make everything smaller and place restrictions on what is available to you.

Being able to take life on, to engage with it instead of being an innocent bystander, requires courage and energy. You either sit back and let life happen to you, or you really start living. If you can get your energy flowing you'll find you can do the things you want, sort out your problems, help other people, make more money and feel more satisfied. Life will feel so much better, which means it's a win/win situation.

So it's important to trust in life, even if at times you can't understand what's happening or why. Practise receiving what's coming, even if it's not quite what you want ... yet. Hold the intention without expectation, and wait without struggling. Say to yourself that you're relaxing into life.

● Realize It's All There for You

The most important thing is to *stop panicking*. We feel there must be a deadline for having what we want, but cosmic timing works purely on its own terms. Being graceful, poised and elegant means you can handle anything. Relax from the tension of having to have everything *now* (just like a screaming toddler). You're getting the best there is available at the time. Being grateful is also good news. Otherwise we are caught in a cycle of wanting more and more, and never appreciating what we already have.

The premise of abundant thinking is that there is no shortage at the universal level. There's always enough – it's just that things have difficulty getting through at times.

And the more desperate you are, the more stuck the energy becomes. Desperation is a repelling force. And if you play hard to get then you're blocking off ways for the delivery to get through. *Focus on being warm, anticipatory and relaxed*. That magnetic energy of affinity and attraction works best when you are desirable, so realize that you are and be it!

Once you understand that there is a connection between what is happening to you on the outside and what is going on within you, then you've really got a fantastic tool to play with. Practise with it at first on the small things: intending and imagining a happy day, a parking space, a good meeting, the clothing size you want being in stock. Always affirm what you want – not what you don't want.

Then on a larger scale, when it comes to magnetizing a relationship, this tool will give you the power to change your pattern. You will see that the threat or the opportunity is *in you* and not out there after all. You can start choosing to be what you want and to stop behaving automatically.

Develop Your Personal Awareness

● Release the Tension

A Buddhist monk once taught me the importance of doing 'Living Meditations'. We don't need to adopt special poses or perform rituals to get in touch with the power of reflection. We can go outside and just look up into the night sky. See ourselves as a mere speck in the universe and recognize that there is more to life than our problems. We can walk by a river and let the flow of the water soothe us as we realize that 'this too will pass'.

We can also take deep breaths and calm ourselves down. When you hold on to your breath your whole system starts to shut down. Simply by breathing deeply and evenly we can remind ourselves of the flow, the connection between taking in and letting out. You can cleanse and clear yourself, and effect a huge letting go by breathing out your internal toxic energy in a big whoosh of breath. Feel the release in your body and let the tension drop away.

It's easy to forget how much choice we have over how we feel at any given moment.

- We can't choose what happens to us all the time, but we can always choose how we respond.

- We have so many thoughts, memories and 'things to do' buzzing around in our minds that we feel fragmented and exhausted. Clearing the chatter in your head is vital for effective cosmic ordering and internal well-being.

- The way you carry yourself is a dead give-away of what's going on inside you. It also transmits huge messages to others.

THE BODILY GIVE-AWAYS

- Not looking someone in the eye – conveys a lack of connection
- A knee constantly vibrating up and down – indicates nervous energy or impatience
- Hunched shoulders – shows a need for self-protection or a feeling of being burdened
- Looking rigid – means you are uptight or tense

OPENING UP AND CLOSING DOWN

Imagine you are a flower. First visualize yourself as a closed bud, holding all your colour, perfume and glory inside you. Then slowly imagine yourself opening up into a flower; notice each petal unfold. When you are at full stretch enjoy the feeling of being radiantly open and available for all to see. You are in your prime. Then watch the petals slowly close up again, one by one, until you are back to being a tight bud. You have complete control over when to open and when to close. Practise!

To be able to stay emotionally open requires you to be open in your body and your mind. But what about protecting ourselves? We don't want to be sitting targets for someone's else's negative energy. You can practise opening up and closing down with this simple visualization.

● **Our Choices**

● We can *choose to see our projections*: where we superimpose ourselves (usually the parts we don't want to acknowledge) on to someone else. *That person is mean, tricky, etc.* We attribute our unconscious desires and impulses to someone else. Once we realize that our perception of whether something is positive or negative is up to us, then we don't need to spend our time and energy in judging the other person, but are able to get on with our own lives. It's all a projection anyway and we can decide either way – and then we've got a lot more power over our lives.

● We can *choose to see a crisis as an opportunity*. The Chinese word for crisis is *wei-chi*, which joins together the concept of crisis and opportunity. We may have a problem on our hands, but if we insist on viewing it as a difficulty then we will lose out on the opportunity that's contained within it. *In the end it's not what actually happens to us, but what we think about what happens to us that counts.*

● We can *choose to intend* to attract what we want and do something positive about it. By the way, procrastination is the opposite of intention.

● We can *choose to stay connected* to the cosmos, to ourselves and to each other. Or remember that we *are* all connected. Energy itself is connected, however random and chaotic it seems, so that scientists have even pondered whether a butterfly flapping its wings in Texas could set off a typhoon in Tokyo six days later. But this sense of connection is nothing new. 'All things by immortal power, hiddenly, linked to each other are, For thou can't stir of a flower without the troubling of a star.' (Frances Thompson)

● We can *choose to travel light*: 'Dance like nobody's watching, love like you've never been hurt, sing like nobody's listening, live like it's heaven on earth.' (Mark Twain)

● We can *choose to accept*. Acceptance gives you the most power to do anything you want. It is the pivot and is surprisingly dynamic. It does not mean that you have to forget, or that you agree with someone's behaviour or something that's happened. But the act of acceptance contains magical potency. It means that internally you can change and rearrange your own reactions and live life in a state of peacefulness. Sometimes (*but don't count on it!*) the whole situation is transformed.

● Raise Your Energy Levels

Occasionally we talk about it being 'one of those days', when nothing seems to go right. Or of being 'on a roll', when seemingly we can do nothing wrong. Whatever the cause of this, whether it's a run of luck, difficult energy, static interference, a series of mishaps stemming from carelessness or a string of opportunities that all come together, we are realizing that the timing is either right or wrong and that we can work with it.

Making yourself aware of when it's not the right time means you can conserve energy and direct it to where you can make best use of it. For instance, if you try and make a phone call to a certain person or organization several times but find you're not getting through – either they are constantly engaged or are unavailable – then this is a message from the universe. Leave it! You will only waste time and energy if you continue trying to make that call. If you wait until another day you'll often find that you get through straight away. You might choose to be *dynamic* and keep plugging away, in the Alan Sugar modus operandi, but this is really your ego trying to assert its superiority over the universal flow of energy. Alternatively, you might choose to be *receptive* to the signals. To do something else with your time and wait until the weak energy is strengthened and starts to flow again.

You can get what you want by being still.

The same goes for when you're out shopping for something. No matter where you go or what you try on it isn't quite right, doesn't look good on you or they don't have it in your size. You can pick this up very quickly if it happens twice in a row. Abandon your shopping trip, unless you want to drive yourself crazy and waste time. As you open up your energy you'll quickly read what's in the atmosphere. Whether there's an energy low or an energy high, you will read the signals and get the message.

We are so used to being stressed, to having 'the buzz', that we lose the ability to be still. So much emphasis is placed on 'being busy' that only extrovert activity gains any kudos in our twenty-first-century mindset. In fact, we now wear our stress like a badge of achievement to show how important, needed, busy and successful we are. Then, when we do finally have some time off, our bodies are unable to relax. Actually it takes a lot more energy to be uptight than it does to be relaxed. Being so busy steals and saps our energy. And it robs us of a still place where we can connect to the universe.

Of course, energy responds well to a better diet and a cleaner, tidier, quieter environment. We are addicted to media, to being 'in touch' with each other through impersonal means such as texting. Bombarding each other and becoming invaded by shocking media headlines depletes our pure energy. If we constantly soak up bad news on television, read mindless trash and gossip about people then our good energy gets depleted. Just be aware of what's going on in your environment. You can use feng shui to clear your space.

THE VOID SPACE

Sometimes we're thrown into a void space. The tube train is stuck in the tunnel, the bus won't come, the person we're meeting is running late. This is not a waste of time! These are opportunities to go into the void and mentally rebalance, or reconnect with what we want – and then put out a few wishes.

And Finally

We are all searchers – looking for someone or something to make us feel complete. So often we imagine another person will make us feel this way, but we can really only find this feeling from within. And the mere mention of 'finding it within' can make us feel empty, as we mentally check our stomach cavities and realize that all that's in there is a tin of baked beans, or some Goji berries (if we're the healthy sort), but certainly not an eternal and abundant supply of bliss and happiness. So where is this bliss?

Ancient Taoist wisdom talks about 'the source' from which all things come and to which all things return. Everything comes from here, whether it's a handbag, a hot dog or a happy smile. Being able to access this place is your ticket to happiness. And the more frequently you go there, partake of it and bring it into your life, the happier you will be. No matter what happens. Being able to connect with that vast floating abundance is your chance to recharge, and it's the closest thing to heaven available on earth. It is your permanently available source of security – you can plug into it at any time ... *it's up to you!*